PIANO•VOCAL•GUITAR

Queen
DELUXE ANTHOLOGY

ISBN 978-0-7935-3617-7

HAL•LEONARD®
CORPORATION
7777 W. BLUEMOUND RD. P.O. BOX 13819 MILWAUKEE, WI 53213

WE WILL ROCK YOU

Words and Music by
BRIAN MAY

1. Bud-dy you're a   boy   make a big   noise play-in' in the
2. Bud-dy you're a young   man,   hard man shout-in' in the
3. Bud-dy you're an old   man,   poor man plead-in' with your

street gon-na be a   big man some   day you got   mud   on yo'   face   you   big dis-grace
street gon-na take on   the world some   day you got   blood   on yo'   face   you   big dis-grace
eyes   gon-na make you some peace some day you got   mud   on your   face   you   big dis-grace, Some-

kick-in' your   can ___ all o-ver the   place sing-in'
wav-in' your   ban-ner all o-ver the   place sing-in'   } We will we will rock you ___ we will we will   rock you. ___
bod-y   bet-ter put you back in-to your place sing-in'

We will we will rock you   We will we will rock you.   We will we will

rock you.

Play 3 times

WE ARE THE CHAMPIONS

Words and Music by
FREDDIE MERCURY

KILLER QUEEN

Words and Music by
FREDDIE MERCURY

10

RADIO GA GA

Words and Music by
ROGER TAYLOR

FAT BOTTOMED GIRLS

Words and Music by
BRIAN MAY

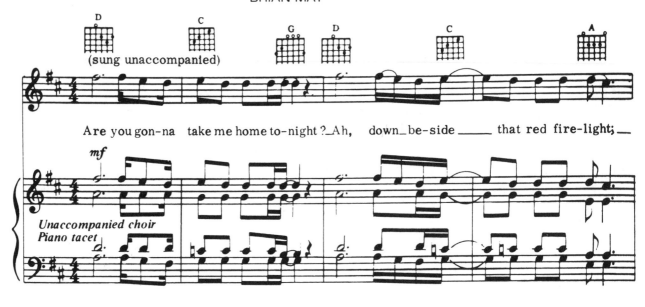

(sung unaccompanied)

Are you gon-na take me home to-night? Ah, down be-side that red fire-light;

mf

Unaccompanied choir
Piano tacet

are you gon-na let it all hang out? Fat bot-tomed girls, you make the rock-in' world go

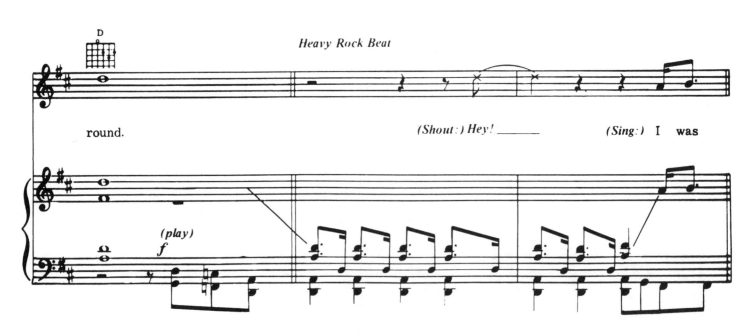

round.

Heavy Rock Beat

(Shout:) Hey! _____

(Sing:) I was

(play)

f

18

I WANT TO BREAK FREE

Words and Music by
JOHN DEACON

TEAR IT UP

Words and Music by
BRIAN MAY

Are you rea - dy?   Well are you   rea - dy?

3 times

Give me your mind, ba - by, give me your bo - dy.

27

30

SAVE ME

Words and Music by
BRIAN MAY

33

IT'S LATE

Words and Music by
BRIAN MAY

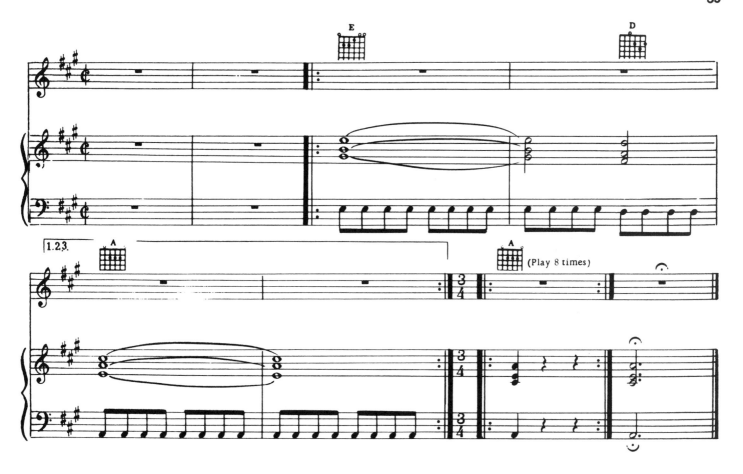

2. The way you love me
    is the sweetest love around.
    But after all this time, the more I'm trying,
    The more I seem to let you down.
    Now you tell me you're leaving, and I
    just can't believe it's true.
    Oh you know that I can love you
    though you know I can't be true.
    Oh you make me love you,
    don't tell me that we're through.
    It's late and it's driving me so mad.
    It's late, but don't try to tell me that
    It's too late save our love you can't turn out the light,
    So late, I've been wrong but I'll learn to be right.
    It's late, it's late, it's late, but not too late.

3. You're starting at me
    with suspicion in your eye.
    You say what game you're playing, what's this
    that you're saying, I know that I can't reply.
    If I take you to-night is it making my life a lie.
    Oh you make me wonder, did I live my life alright.
    It's late, but it's time to set me free.
    It's late, oh yes I know but there's no way it has to be
    Too late, so let the fire take our bodies this night
    So late, so let the waters take our guilt in the tide.

SOMEBODY TO LOVE

Words and Music by
FREDDIE MERCURY

41

44

45

NEED YOUR LOVING TONIGHT

Words and Music by
JOHN DEACON

ANOTHER ONE BITES THE DUST

Words and Music by
JOHN DEACON

1. Steve walks wa - ri - ly down the street with the
2. How do you think I'm going to get a - long with -
% There are plen - ty of ways you can hurt a man, and

brim pulled way down low. Ain't no sound but the sound of his feet; ma -
out you, when you're gone? You took me for e - 'vry - thing that I had and
bring him to the ground. You can beat him you can cheat him you can treat him bad and

FLASH'S THEME a/k/a FLASH

Words and Music by
BRIAN MAY

Just a man ___ with a man's cou-rage. ___ He knows, ___ noth-ing but a man, ___ but he can nev-er fail. ___

No one but the pure in heart ___ may find the gold-en ___ grail oh oh ___ oh oh. ___

Tempo I

SPOKEN:— Flash, Flash, I love you,

but we on-ly have four-teen hours to save the Earth. Flash.

(1st time only)

Repeat and Fade

BODY LANGUAGE

Words and Music by
FREDDIE MERCURY

You've got the cut-est ass ____ I've ev-er seen,__ knock me

down for a six ____ an-y time. ____

Look at me, ____

I got-ta case of bod-y lan - guage;--   look at me,__

of bod-y lan - guage; ____   of bod-y lan - guage. ____

D.S. al Coda

Coda

hot!

N.C.

mp

f

Bod - y lan - guage.   Bod - y

Repeat ad lib and Fade

mf

3. *Sexy body;*
   Sexy, sexy body.
   I want your body.
   Baby, you're hot!

   (To Coda)

DON'T STOP ME NOW

Words and Music by
FREDDIE MERCURY

YOU'RE MY BEST FRIEND

Words and Music by
JOHN DEACON

72

UNDER PRESSURE

Words and Music by FREDDIE MERCURY, JOHN DEACON,
BRIAN MAY, ROGER TAYLOR and DAVID BOWIE

Moderately

(Voice tacet 1st time)
Bah bah bah bah, bah bah bah bah bah bah bah bah bah bah.

1. Pres - sure, push - ing down_ on me; press - ing
2.(See additional lyrics)

down_ on you;_ no man ask for. Un - der pres - sure, that burns

76

Verse 2:

Chippin' around,
Kick my brains around the floor.
These are the days it never rains but it pours.
(vocal ad lib)
People on streets.
People on streets.

I'M IN LOVE WITH MY CAR

Words and Music by
ROGER TAYLOR

Slowly (in 2)

The ma-chine of a dream.___

Such a clean ma-chine,___   With the pis-tons a-pump-in',

And the hub-caps all gleam.   When I'm hold-ing your wheel,

82

BICYCLE RACE

Words and Music by
FREDDIE MERCURY

LONG AWAY

Words and Music by
BRIAN MAY

92

BOHEMIAN RHAPSODY

Words and Music by
FREDDIE MERCURY

99

GOOD OLD-FASHIONED LOVER BOY

Words and Music by
FREDDIE MERCURY

love you.___ Hey boy, where did you get___ it from? Hey boy, where did you go?___ I

learned my pas - sion in the good old - fash - ioned school of lov - er

boy.

Instrumental Solo

D. C. al Fine

KEEP YOURSELF ALIVE

Words and Music by
BRIAN MAY

1. I was told a mil-lion times of all the trou-bles in my way, Tried to
2. Well, I've loved a mil-lion wom-en in a bel-la-don-ic haze, And I

grow a lit-tle wis-er, lit-tle bet-ter ev-'ry day; But if I crossed a mil-lion riv-ers and I
ate a mil-lion din-ners brought to me on sil-ver Trays; Give me ev-'ry-thing I need to feed my

D.C. 1st time
Segue 2nd time

Keep your-self a - live, ___ It - 'll take you all your time and a-mon-ey, hon-ey, you'll sur - vive.

Keep your - self a - live, keep your - self a - live, ___ It - 'll take you all your time and a - mon-ey to

IT'S A HARD LIFE

Words and Music by
FREDDIE MERCURY

CHORUS

love. ____

back on my-self and say__ I did it for love ____ Yes I did it for love, _____ for

love.   Oh _____   I did it for love. _____

CALLING ALL GIRLS

Words and Music by
ROGER TAYLOR

'39

Words and Music by
BRIAN MAY

123

PLAY THE GAME

Words and Music by
FREDDIE MERCURY

129

TIE YOUR MOTHER DOWN

Words and Music by
BRIAN MAY

With a rock beat

Get your par - ty gown,— and get your pig-tail down,— and get your

heart beat - in', ba - by.— Got my tim - in' right,— and got my

act all tight,— It's got to be to-night, my lit-tle school babe. Your

mom-ma says you don't, And your dad-dy says you won't, And I'm boil-in' up in-side, Ain't no way

CRAZY LITTLE THING CALLED LOVE

Medium Shuffle Beat

Words and Music by
FREDDIE MERCURY

BRIGHTON ROCK

Words and Music by
BRIAN MAY

no, I'm com-pro-mised, I must a-pol-o-gise, If my

la-dy should dis-cov-er how I spent my hol-i-days."